34886000823307

BOOK CHARGING CARD

Accession No. _____ Call No. _9768_ _SEM_

Author _Semchuk, Rosann_

Title _Tennessee_

Date

Semchuk, Rosann
Tennessee

34880000823307

TENNESSEE

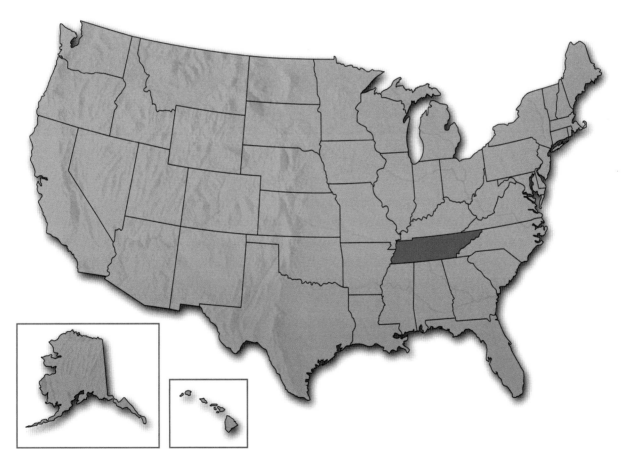

Rosann Semchuk

Published by Weigl Publishers Inc.
123 South Broad Street, Box 227
Mankato, MN   56002
USA
Web site: http://www.weigl.com

Library of Congress Cataloging-in-Publication Data available upon request from the publisher. Fax: (507) 388-2746 for the attention of the Publishing Records Department.

ISBN 1-930954-79-4

Printed in the United States of America
1 2 3 4 5 6 7 8 9 10   05 04 03 02 01

Editor
Jennifer Nault
Copy Editor
Kara Turner
Designers
Warren Clark
Terry Paulhus
Katherine Phillips
Photo Researchers
Diana Marshall
Gayle Murdoff

Photograph Credits

Every reasonable effort has been made to trace ownership and to obtain permission to reprint copyright material. The publishers would be pleased to have any errors or omissions brought to their attention so that they may be corrected in subsequent printings.

Cover: Cotton (Cheraw Visitors Bureau), saxophone player (Memphis Convention and Visitors Bureau), **Bettman/Corbis:** page 19B; **Bristol Motor Speedway:** page 27T; **Corel Corporation:** pages 3M, 3B, 10T, 11B, 14T, 28T, 28B, 29L, 29R; **Charlene Faris:** page 18T; **Kentucky Historical Society:** page 18B; **Memphis Convention and Visitors Bureau:** pages 4B, 5T, 15B, 20T, 22T, 24T, 24B; **Mississippi Department of Archives and History:** page 17T; **New Hampshire Historical Society:** page 17B; **PhotoDisc Corporation:** pages 13T, 27B; **Photofest:** page 25T; **J&D Richardson Photography:** pages 3T, 4T, 6T, 6B, 8T, 8B, 9T, 9B, 10BR, 11T, 13B, 15T, 21T, 21B, 22B; **Chase Swift/ Corbis:** page 7B; **Tennessee Tourist Development:** pages 7T, 12T, 12B, 20B, 23T, 23B, 25B, 26T, 26B; **Tennessee Valley Authority:** page 14B; **The Tennessee Secretary of State:** pages 10BL, 21BL; **Women's Basketball Hall of Fame/Wes Cate:** page 27BL; **Marilyn "Angel" Wynn:** pages 16T, 16B.

CONTENTS

INTRODUCTION

With more than 800 miles of trails in the Great Smoky Mountains National Park, hiking and camping enthusiasts are sure to find adventure.

If you have an ear for the "blues," Tennessee is the place to visit. Memphis, the most populated city in Tennessee, was an important location during the blues music craze that occurred in the United States during the 1930s. Beale Street was Memphis's main music district, made famous by blues composer W. C. Handy. Known as "The Father of the Blues," Handy released his first song, "Memphis Blues," in 1912. The blues, a style of African-American folk music, was relatively unknown to many people in the United States. Handy's songs and Beale Street brought these soulful tunes into the limelight. In fact, Memphis is mentioned in many popular blues songs.

Although the name *Tennessee* is synonymous with the blues, it also brings to mind the Great Smoky Mountains, the American Civil War, Davy Crockett, Elvis Presley, and Nashville.

Blues legend B. B. King opened a blues club in Memphis in 1991.

QUICK FACTS

Nashville is the capital of Tennessee.

Music played such a large role in Tennessee's history that it has the most state songs in the nation. There are six official state songs. They are: "The Tennessee Waltz," "Tennessee, My Homeland," "Tennessee," "When it's Iris Time in Tennessee," "My Tennessee," and "Rocky Top."

With 5.7 million people, Tennessee ranks 17th in population in the United States.

The Copper Basin in Tennessee is so different from the surrounding area that it has been recognized by astronauts from space. The barren landscape was caused by mining in the nineteenth century.

Tennessee's railroad system is extensive, with 2,695 miles of tracks.

Tennessee's rivers all lie within the Mississippi River system.

Nashville International Airport is the nation's thirty-seventh busiest airport.

The largest earthquake in the history of the United States occurred in Tennessee. Known as the New Madrid Earthquake, it shocked the residents of Tennessee during the winter of 1811. It helped form Reelfoot Lake, located in the northwest.

Until the 1940s, farming was the most important economic activity in the state.

More National Guard soldiers were deployed from Tennessee for the Gulf War effort than any other state.

Nashville's original name was Fort Nashborough.

Getting There

The state of Tennessee is bordered by the Appalachian Mountains on the east and the Mississippi River on the west. It shares its borders with eight other states. Kentucky lies to the north, and Virginia, North Carolina, and South Carolina border the east. Georgia, Alabama, and Mississippi lie to the south, and Arkansas and Missouri border the west.

The key transportation centers in Tennessee are Memphis, Nashville, Knoxville, and Chattanooga. Barges navigate the Tennessee River, but the state's main port is on the Mississippi River, near Memphis.

Tennessee has 86,000 miles of highways and roads. The main highway in Tennessee is Interstate 40, an east–west route that links the state's main cities. Large freeways that run north–south include Interstates 24, 65, and 75.

The Memphis trolley system transports more than 800,000 passengers per year.

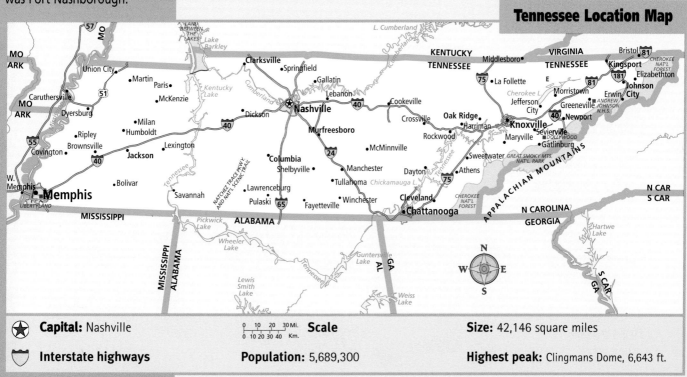

Tennessee Location Map

Capital: Nashville

Interstate highways

Scale
0 10 20 30 Mi.
0 10 20 30 40 Km.

Population: 5,689,300

Size: 42,146 square miles

Highest peak: Clingmans Dome, 6,643 ft.

As the site of many major battles during the American Civil War, Tennessee commemorates this important historical period by staging re-enactments.

Tennessee's name attests to the historical significance of the Native Peoples in the state. The name *Tennessee* is derived from a Cherokee word, *Tanasi.* It means "a bend in the river." Tanasi was a major Cherokee village. It was situated on the banks of the Tennessee River, a river that bends to such an extent that it flows through the state twice.

Over the years, Tennessee has been given several nicknames, but the most popular is "The Volunteer State." The nickname originated during the War of 1812. Many brave volunteer soldiers from Tennessee fought in the Battle of New Orleans, under General Andrew Jackson. These soldiers prevented the English from gaining access to the Mississippi Valley. This battle marked the beginning of Tennessee's great military tradition.

Tennessee is often considered a divider state between the North and the South. During the American Civil War, Tennessee's loyalties were divided as well. Tennessee was the last state to leave the Union and the first to return.

QUICK FACTS

Tennessee became the sixteenth state to join the Union on June 1, 1796.

The Green County Courthouse has a monument that honors both the Union and Confederate armies. It is the only monument of its kind in the United States.

Shelby County has more horses per person than any other county in the United States.

Pioneer Davy Crockett was born near Greeneville. A replica of his log cabin stands there today.

The raccoon is Tennessee's state animal.

The Great Smoky Mountains encompass 800 square miles and are almost entirely covered by forests.

Nearly two-fifths of Tennessee is **rural**, and the state's economy was, until recently, largely based upon agriculture. Although some Tennesseans still work on farms, most people work in offices, retail outlets, and factories. Tennessee became more **industrialized** during the twentieth century. The state's largest move toward industrialization occurred in the 1930s. This decade saw the development of the Tennessee River basin under the Tennessee Valley Authority (TVA). The TVA programs attracted a great number of diverse industries, such as the federal government's atomic energy research and development center at Oak Ridge.

Although the state has changed over the years, it has retained much of its original charm. Tennessee is still a picturesque state known for its friendly people, rich musical origins, and lush, forested mountains.

Tennessee's country music originated deep in the Appalachian Mountains.

Nashville covers Davidson County—an area of 530 square miles. This makes it one of the nation's largest cities.

LAND AND CLIMATE

Tennessee features a rich assortment of plants and animals. Many species are protected by parks and wildlife sanctuaries.

Tennessee has six main land regions. From east to west, these regions are: the Blue Ridge region, the Appalachian Ridge and Valley Region, the Appalachian Plateau, the Highland Rim, the Nashville Basin, and the Gulf Coastal Plain. Each area is distinct. For instance, the Blue Ridge region, located along the eastern edge of Tennessee, has an average elevation of 5,000 feet. It is here that Clingmans Dome, the state's tallest peak, rises to 6,643 feet.

The largest rivers in the state are the Mississippi, Tennessee, and Cumberland rivers. The Mississippi River drains most of west Tennessee. Its largest **tributaries** in the state include the Forked Deer, Hatchie, Loosahatchie, Obion, and Wolf rivers. The rest of the state is drained mostly by the Cumberland and Tennessee Rivers.

Tennessee's climate is hot in the summer and mild in the winter. Snowfall is light in the central and western parts of Tennessee, but it is often heavy in the eastern mountains.

NATURAL RESOURCES

Tennessee has fertile soils, a vast supply of water, and an abundance of minerals. The state's most fertile soils are found in the Appalachian Ridge and Valley Region, the Nashville Basin, and the Gulf Coastal Plain. Fertile soils consisting of sand, silt, and clay also cover the Mississippi Alluvial Plain. The Appalachian Plateau and much of the Highland Rim, however, have poor-quality soils.

Beneath the soil, there are many valuable minerals. In the east, there are large deposits of marble, pyrite, and zinc. In the center of the state, limestone and zinc are found. Coal deposits can be found around the Appalachian Plateau. Coal fields cover about 5,000 square miles of Tennessee.

Forestry is another economic activity that depends upon Tennessee's natural resources. Nationally, the state ranks second in the production of hardwood lumber. Tennessee's 14.4 million acres of forests support a healthy $17 billion forestry industry.

Tennessee greatly values its water supplies, with many programs protecting the state's streams, lakes, and rivers.

QUICK FACTS

Tennessee has 926 square miles of inland water.

Crushed stone, zinc, cement, sand, gravel, and clay are common minerals found in Tennessee.

Limestone, which is found in large amounts in Tennessee, was declared the official state rock in 1979.

Water is a precious natural resource. **Hydroelectricity** provides more than 125 billion kilowatt-hours of electricity.

About 75 percent of the state's coal is taken from underground mines.

Tennessee ranks first in the nation in the production of hardwood flooring and pencils.

Marble, sandstone, clay, sand, and gravel account for about 45 percent of the state's annual mineral production value.

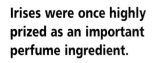

Irises were once highly prized as an important perfume ingredient.

PLANTS AND ANIMALS

About 55 percent of Tennessee is forested. This is a significant improvement since the 1920s, when only 36 percent of the state was forested. Hardwoods make up most of the state's trees. The most common tree species, in descending order, are: soft maples, white oaks, hickories, blackgums (tupelos), and red cedars. The forests of eastern Tennessee include red spruces and Fraser firs, while western Tennessee forests include black willows,cottonwoods, and silver maples.

The bald cypress is common in the low swampy bottomlands of western Tennessee. Big Cypress Tree State Park was once home to the largest and oldest bald cypress tree in the United States. This cone-bearing hardwood was 175-feet tall and 40 feet in **circumference**. Unfortunately, the tree was struck by lightning in 1976, ending its 1,350-year-old life.

QUICK FACTS

The iris is the state flower. The state wildflower is the passion flower.

The state gem is the river pearl, which is found in the shells of freshwater mussels. River pearls come in various shapes and colors.

The state tree of Tennessee is the tulip poplar.

Shrubs and flowering trees in the state include red flame azaleas, mountain laurels, dogwoods, and rhododendrons.

Cypress trees in swampy areas often have unusual growths that are commonly referred to as "knees." One theory suggests that the knees help carry oxygen to the roots of the cypress.

Quick Facts

Tennessee fish include black bass, carp, perch, and catfish.

In 1995, the Tennessee cave salamander was named the official state amphibian, and the eastern box turtle was named the official state reptile.

Many types of birds can be found in Tennessee year-round, including robins, eastern bluebirds, mockingbirds, and chickadees. Birds that live in Tennessee during the summer months include warblers, sparrows, hawks, and swallows.

The Mississippi Flyway, in the western portion of the state, is used by millions of birds as a migratory route.

Tennessee has two official state insects: the firefly and the ladybug.

Black bears roam remote parts of Tennessee's Great Smoky Mountains. Black bear populations in the Great Smoky Mountains rose dramatically in the late 1990s, with an estimated 1,800 now living in the area. It is believed that the Great Smoky Mountains National Park contains about 15 percent of all the black bears in North America. When they are tracking prey, black bears can run as fast as 25 miles per hour. They are also skillful at climbing trees.

The shell of a turtle is called a carapace. The eastern box turtle has a carapace with colorful concentric rings.

Small mammals in Tennessee are abundant and include beavers, muskrats, rabbits, raccoons, skunks, and squirrels. The flying squirrel, found in Tennessee, is the smallest type of tree squirrel. This tiny animal is mostly **nocturnal**. The flying squirrel has a fold of skin that stretches from its front leg to its rear leg on both sides of its body. When a flying squirrel stretches out its legs, the folds of skin become taut and form "wings." This excess skin allows the squirrel to glide distances of up to 150 feet.

Flying squirrels are about 9 to 10 inches long, including their tail.

Graceland, the late Elvis Presley's estate, features a 23-room mansion. It is one of the most visited buildings in the United States.

TOURISM

Every year, millions of tourists come to Tennessee with music on their minds. Nashville and Memphis draw many visitors interested in discovering the state's musical heritage. Elvis Presley's home is preserved in Memphis. Elvis lived on a 14-acre estate called Graceland. Today, visitors can tour the lavish mansion. The highlight of the mansion tour is Elvis's trophy room, which houses his gold records, awards, and career mementos.

On a different musical note is Nashville, home to the Grand Ole Opry. This live country-music show has hosted talented country performers since 1925. Today, the Grand Ole Opry features contemporary and traditional country-music performances.

Country superstar Dolly Parton, from Locust Ridge, never forgot her Tennessee roots. Her theme park, Dollywood, is nestled near the Great Smoky Mountains National Park. Dollywood features music, crafts, attractions, and rides. It also stages country-music concerts throughout the year.

Dolly Parton wrote her first song at 5 years of age and appeared on the Grand Ole Opry when she was just 13 years old.

QUICK FACTS

Tennessee is known for its caverns, including Jewel Cave near Tennessee City. This natural wonder contains beautiful rock formations and fossils.

The Tennessee Aquarium in Chattanooga is the world's largest freshwater aquarium. It contains more than 9,000 animals.

The Nashville Toy Museum has hundreds of trains on display, along with antique dolls, bears, toy soldiers, and a large model boat and ship collection.

More than 2,800 animals are housed in the Memphis Zoo.

Tennessee is home to many historical landmarks, including the Hermitage, near Nashville. The Hermitage was the home of the seventh president of the United States, Andrew Jackson.

Almost 25 percent of the total value of all goods and services produced in Tennessee each year comes from manufacturing.

INDUSTRY

Agriculture is a vital industry to the state's economy. There are approximately 89,000 farms in Tennessee. The most common crops grown in the state include cotton, corn, soybeans, strawberries, and tobacco. Cotton, which is grown in the western part of the state, ranks as Tennessee's leading crop. In eastern Tennessee, there are many livestock farms. Livestock farmers raise a variety of animals, including cattle, hogs, chickens, and sheep. Beef cattle are the leading source of income in the livestock industry.

Tennessee's main manufactured products are chemicals, transportation equipment, processed foods and beverages, and machinery. The five largest industrial employers are Lockheed Martin Energy Systems, Tennessee Eastman, Nissan Motor Manufacturing Corporation, Oak Ridge National Laboratory, and Saturn Corporation. Saturn, an automobile company, was formed in 1985. Based in Spring Hill, Saturn employs 7,800 people, who assemble sedans and station wagons.

QUICK FACTS

Since the 1990s, Tennessee has become a major manufacturer of automobiles and metal products.

Crops are grown on 59 percent of Tennessee's farmland.

Tennessee is a major supplier of marble in the United States, exporting more than 270,000 tons per year.

Lockheed Martin Energy Systems employs 4,165 people in Tennessee.

The growing season lasts from 150 days in northeastern Tennessee to more than 230 days in the southwest.

Tomatoes and snap beans are the most important vegetables grown in the state.

About 60,000 people work in forestry-related jobs in Tennessee.

The Mississippi River is the nation's chief inland waterway. The river ranges in depth from 9 feet to 100 feet and is about 3.5 miles at its widest point.

The TVA manages twenty-one reservoir systems in Tennessee and is responsible for 175,000 acres of land near the reservoirs.

GOODS AND SERVICES

When it comes to electric power, Tennessee is well supplied. In 1933, the Tennessee Valley Authority (TVA) was created to develop the natural resources of the area and as a job-creation program. The TVA built dams and harnessed water power to create electricity. Over the years, the TVA has contributed greatly to the state's prosperity and to Tennessee's transition from an agricultural- to an industrial-based economy. Today, twenty-nine of the fifty dams controlled by the TVA generate electricity. The TVA also operates eleven coal-burning power plants. Together, they provide the largest source of electricity produced by the TVA. The TVA headquarters are in Knoxville.

Power generated by the TVA is distributed over an area of about 80,000 square miles, serving a population of more than 7 million people. This area includes Tennessee and parts of Alabama, Virginia, Georgia, Kentucky, North Carolina, and Mississippi. The TVA produces more power than any other power system in the nation.

QUICK FACTS

Tennessee's flag has three stars which represent the different land forms in Tennessee: mountains, highlands, and lowlands.

The distance between Memphis and Nashville is 210 miles.

Coca-Cola was first bottled in 1899 in Chattanooga.

The first public library in Tennessee was opened in Nashville in 1813. Today, Tennessee has about 250 public libraries.

Tennessee has about 160 newspapers in circulation. Popular newspapers include *The Chattanooga Free Press, The Chattanooga Times,* and *The Knoxville News-Sentinel.*

About 9,100 people are employed by the TVA in the state of Tennessee.

The University of Tennessee, in Knoxville, was founded in 1794. Today, more than 20,000 students attend the university.

Community, business, and personal services are the most important sectors in Tennessee's service industry. Of Tennessee's 2.8 million employed residents, the largest percentage, 28 percent, work in tourism. Another 22 percent work in retail. The state government also employs a large number of Tennesseans.

Economic activities in the service industry include private health care, business services, and universities. Johnson City, Memphis, and Nashville are important health centers in Tennessee. They each support large hospitals and colleges of medicine. In business, FedEx Corporation, a company that specializes in mail delivery and information technology, has a large base in Memphis. FedEx Corporation is the state's largest private employer. Tennessee has twenty-five public colleges and universities and fifty-eight private post-secondary institutions. The major universities are the University of Tennessee, Vanderbilt University, Fisk University, and Tennessee State University.

QUICK FACTS

There are 16.5 students for every teacher in Tennessee.

Seventy-seven percent of Tennessee residents over the age of 25 years hold a high-school diploma.

Fisk University is the oldest university in Nashville. Founded in 1866, it began as a place of education for newly freed slaves.

Tennessee spends an average of $4,548 on each student's education. Education is mandatory for children between the ages of 7 and 17 years. About 11 percent of children in the state attend private schools.

Levi Strauss, a clothing manufacturing company, employs 900 people in Knoxville.

The *Memphis Queen II* was Memphis's first all-steel passenger vessel.

FIRST NATIONS

The word "Cherokee" is derived from the term *Ani-Yun-wiya*, which means "the principle people."

Native Peoples have been living in Tennessee for at least 11,000 years. About 2,000 years ago, the Woodland culture grew crops, built mounds, and made clay pottery. Mounds from this period still exist in many parts of Tennessee. Native Peoples that have called Tennessee home include the Chickasaw, the Yuchi, and the Cherokee, all of whom settled along the banks of Tennessee's major rivers. The Cherokee and the Chickasaw were the most powerful groups. The Cherokee lived and hunted in eastern Tennessee, near the upper area of the Tennessee River, and the Chickasaw inhabited western Tennessee. Both groups claimed the middle portion of the state, and clashed over this territory until the nineteenth century.

Spanish explorers were the first Europeans to reach Tennessee, but their contact with the Native Peoples had unfortunate consequences. The Spanish introduced new diseases and many Native Peoples died from the spread of these diseases. By the time the French entered Tennessee in the late 1600s, the Native-American population was greatly reduced.

QUICK FACTS

One of Tennessee's official state flowers, the passion flower, is also known by its Native-American name, the *ocoee*.

In the early 1700s, the Yuchi were driven out of the Tennessee area and moved south.

When Spanish explorer Hernando de Soto first came across the Chickasaw, he recorded their name as *Chicaza*.

The Sequoyah Birthplace Museum in Vonore tells the story of Sequoyah. It is dedicated to the history and culture of Native Americans.

The Cherokee alphabet was invented by one person, a man by the name of Chief Sequoyah.

Hernando de Soto was a courageous explorer who helped Spain in its discovery of the New World.

QUICK FACTS

Hernando de Soto was the first European to make contact with the Tennessee Native Americans when he established a winter camp at the town of Chicaza in 1540.

In the late 1600s, English fur traders began to compete with French traders. This led to the French and Indian War.

The largest Native-American groups, the Cherokee and the Chickasaw, fought for England during most of the French and Indian War.

The French and Indian War continued until 1763, when the French surrendered to the English. The French gave the English control of Louisiana, which included present-day Tennessee.

In 1795, Tennessee, which was referred to as the Southwest Territory, had a population of 77,262 people.

EXPLORERS AND MISSIONARIES

Spanish explorers were the first Europeans to enter the Tennessee area. These explorers, led by Hernando de Soto, came across the valley of the Tennessee River in 1540. De Soto traveled farther west and became the first European to reach the Mississippi River. He crossed the Mississippi River in 1541, near the site of present-day Memphis.

Spaniard Juan Pardo explored eastern Tennessee in the 1560s and built several forts in the area, including one near present-day Chattanooga. More than one century later, French explorer René-Robert Cavelier, also known as Sieur de La Salle, claimed the entire Mississippi Valley for France. He did so in 1682. He built a trading post, Fort Prud'homme, on the Chickasaw Bluffs. The post was quickly abandoned due to its isolated location. In 1715, another French trading post, French Lick, was erected near present-day Nashville.

The French and Indian Wars were four wars fought successively between 1689 and 1763. With the support of Native-American allies, these wars resulted in the British gaining control of almost all of North America.

Many early settlers in Tennessee lived in sturdy log cabins.

EARLY SETTLERS

There were permanent settlers living in the Tennessee region by 1769. People from nearby states, namely Virginia and North Carolina, came to the area. The king of England, however, had banned settlers from living in most parts of Tennessee in 1763. Most early settlers simply ignored the ban. By 1769, hundreds of people were living in log cabins along the Watauga River valley. At this time, many settlers still called themselves North Carolinians.

In 1772, a group of settlers formed their own government called the Watauga Association. They drew up the first written constitution west of the Appalachians. Three years later, a group called the Transylvania Company bought a large section of present-day Tennessee and Kentucky from the Cherokee. The Transylvania Company hired a highly regarded pioneer, Daniel Boone, to blaze a trail so that land could be opened to settlers. Boone's trail, named Wilderness Road, served as the main route to the new settlements.

Tennessee's Daniel Boone, who was born on November 2, 1734, is considered a great American hero of the early pioneering tradition.

Many Tennessee settlers supported independence from England and fought in the American Revolution. In 1784, after the war, North Carolina gave up its claim to the Tennessee region. The United States Congress, however, declined to admit the new state. About 10 years later, the people of the area proved that they had a population of 60,000—the requirement for statehood. In 1796, Tennessee adopted a state constitution, chose a governor, and elected Andrew Jackson to Congress. On June 1, 1796, Tennessee became the sixteenth state to join the United States.

The Chickasaw owned nearly all of the western portion of Tennessee. In 1818, however, the Chickasaw **ceded** most of their land to the government. The Cherokee held on to a large tract of land in central Tennessee. They also kept a small portion of land in the east, south of the Little Tennessee and Sequatchie Rivers.

As a young man, Andrew Jackson moved to Tennessee, where he became a successful lawyer and landowner.

QUICK FACTS

In 1862, during the American Civil War, Confederate soldiers attacked General Ulysses S. Grant's troops. This surprise attack at Shiloh resulted in the death of 13,000 Union soldiers and 10,500 Confederate soldiers.

The residents of eastern Tennessee originally planned to name their new state Franklin in honor of former United States President Benjamin Franklin.

Davy Crockett was one of Tennessee's best-known early settlers. Born in 1786, Crockett was a pioneer and a politician. In 1827, he became a member of the United States Congress. Crockett lived near Limestone.

Tennessee's early economy relied heavily upon cotton crops. Today, more than half of the cotton produced in the nation passes through Memphis.

POPULATION

Tennessee has a population of almost 5.7 million people. From 1990 to 2000, the population of Tennessee grew by 16.7 percent—almost 5 percent higher than the national average. Most of this growth occurred in the Nashville Basin. The population of west Tennessee grew very little. Today, the largest city in the state is Memphis, with about 604,000 people. Memphis covers an area of 256 square miles. This southwestern city has a large African-American population, with African Americans making up about 55 percent of the city's residents.

About 25 percent of the population of Tennessee is below the age of 18 years. Residents 65 years of age or older make up slightly more than 12 percent of the population.

More than 60 percent of people in Tennessee live in urban centers.

QUICK FACTS

There are 138 people per square mile in Tennessee. This is far more than the national average of 80 people per square mile.

About 200,000 of the residents of Tennessee work for the state government.

Asian Americans make up 1 percent of the population in Tennessee.

Almost 70 percent of the homes in Tennessee are privately owned. This number is larger than the national figure of 66 percent.

About 16.4 percent of Tennessee's residents are African American. This is significantly greater than the national average of 12 percent.

The Tennessee State Museum focuses on the nation's overseas conflicts, from the Spanish-American War until World War II.

POLITICS AND GOVERNMENT

During the past 200 years, Tennessee has had three different constitutions. The governor of the state serves a four-year term. The state legislature, called the General Assembly, is made up of a thirty-three-member Senate and a ninety-nine-member House of Representatives. Senators serve four-year terms, and house members are elected for two-year terms. The highest court in Tennessee is the state supreme court, which consists of five justices elected for eight-year terms. Most of Tennessee's ninety-five counties are governed by county courts composed of elected justices of the peace. There are 336 **municipalities** in Tennessee, most of which are governed by a mayor and council.

QUICK FACTS

Tennessee's state seal features a plow, a sheaf of wheat, and cotton. These symbols represent the importance of farming to the state. The riverboat highlights the importance of river traffic to the state's economy.

Women obtained the right to vote when Tennessee **ratified** the nineteenth **amendment** to the United States Constitution. This occurred on August 21, 1920.

Shiloh National Military Park and the Shiloh National Cemetery mark the site of the 1862 Battle of Shiloh.

The Tennessee State Capitol is modeled after a temple in Athens, Greece. It is 206 feet tall from the ground to the top of the tower.

CULTURAL GROUPS

African Americans in Tennessee have made significant contributions to the state on many levels—cultural, political, and social. With African Americans making up more than half of Memphis's population, the city is a center of African-American history and heritage. In Tennessee's early days, Memphis operated as a cotton and slave market. Later, in the mid-1900s, Memphis was central to the **civil-rights movement**. Civil-rights leader Doctor Martin Luther King, Jr. was **assassinated** in Memphis in 1968. He is honored today at the National Civil Rights Museum. Located in Memphis, this museum provides an overview of the civil-rights movement through its collections, exhibitions, and educational programs.

Tennessee's first African-American millionaire, Robert R. Church, lived in Memphis. Church was born into slavery but went on to became a political and community leader. In the late 1800s, he helped the city of Memphis during a period of economic hardship by investing in city bonds.

The Brownsville Jazz Festival is a celebration of African-American culture.

Many evangelical religions incorporate clapping, singing, and dancing into their worship.

The Museum of Appalachia is dedicated to celebrating and preserving the rich culture and heritage of those living in the remote hills of the southern Appalachian Mountains.

Tennessee is home to many festivals that honor and preserve the state's traditional southern culture. Since its beginning in a little schoolhouse in 1926, the Appalachian Fair has grown in scope and attendance. Celebrating Tennessee's southern and country music traditions, the Appalachian Fair offers a variety of entertainment every August. Today, more than 250,000 people attend the fair. The main stage welcomes country-music entertainers, such as Marty Stuart and Patty Loveless.

The Memphis in May International Festival is a month-long celebration of local culture and cuisine. Memphis in May hosts the Beale Street Music Festival, the World Championship Barbecue Cooking Contest, and the Great Southern Food Festival.

QUICK FACTS

Memphis musician W. C. Handy is known as "Father of the Blues."

Alex Haley wrote a novel called *Roots*, about an African-American family spanning seven generations. Haley's boyhood home in Henning is a state-owned historic site devoted to African Americans in Tennessee.

In addition to the blues, Tennessee is also known for other types of music, including Appalachian, which is linked to Irish and Scottish musical traditions.

The world's biggest fish-fry is held in Paris, Tennessee every April. More than 12,500 pounds of catfish are fried and served during this event.

The storybook charm of Jonesborough, Tennessee's oldest town, is an ideal setting for the Storytelling Festival that takes place every summer.

ARTS AND ENTERTAINMENT

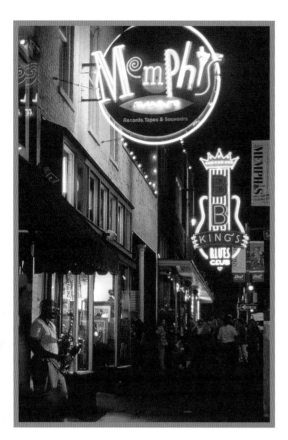

Early Tennessee traditions continue to influence the state's arts and entertainment scenes. Music and southern folk culture are alive throughout the state. Bluegrass music has long been a rural Tennessee tradition, and blues music also has close ties to the state. African Americans have greatly influenced the Memphis music scene, and the city is widely known as the "Home of the Blues." Music legends, such as B. B. King, helped to develop the Memphis blues style. Beale Street in Memphis was, and continues to be, the hub of blues, jazz, and soul music. Today, Beale Street continues this rich musical tradition with a variety of blues nightclubs.

Memphis is home to more than 100 live-music venues, many of which feature talented local artists.

Memphis blues and gospel music greatly influenced Elvis Presley's musical style. Elvis moved to Memphis with his family at the age of 13 years. In 1954, he began his sensational singing career with the Sun Records label in Memphis. Elvis died at his Memphis home, Graceland, on August 16, 1977. Today, the Graceland mansion lures Elvis fans to Tennessee by the millions.

QUICK FACTS

Superstar Tina Turner was born in Memphis in 1939. She won a Grammy Award in 1972 and starred in many movies, including *Mad Max Beyond Thunderdome*.

Cybill Shepherd is from Memphis. She starred in the television series *Moonlighting* and later had her own television show called *Cybill*.

Elvis Presley had a national hit single while recording for the Sun Records label in Memphis. It was called "Mystery Train."

As well as being a talented singer, Elvis Presley starred in thirty-three Hollywood films.

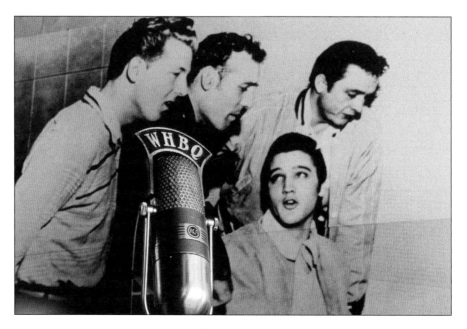

Elvis Presley's first recording studio was Sun Studio in Memphis.

Many of today's celebrities and entertainers hail from the Volunteer State. Actor Morgan Freeman and singer Aretha Franklin are both from Memphis. Aretha Franklin began singing church music at an early age and recorded her first album at the age of 14 years. She has since recorded many soul music albums and is perhaps best known for her song, "Respect." Morgan Freeman has been acting for many years and first appeared in the children's educational television program *The Electric Company.* Since then, Freeman has become a Hollywood celebrity. In 1989, Freeman received an Academy Award nomination for Best Actor for his performance in the film *Driving Miss Daisy.*

For young people who enjoy the theater scene, the Nashville Children's Theater is the place to be. It began providing children's entertainment in the 1930s and continues to thrill more than 85,000 children every year with its energetic performances.

Actor Morgan Freeman, born in Memphis, has appeared in more than twenty-nine films.

QUICK FACTS

Since 1981, the Nashville Opera Association has performed dozens of shows. It is Tennessee's largest opera company.

The Blues City Cultural Center stages plays and musicals about the African-American experience in the South. Its largest production, *Down on Beale*, is about the dance and music scene of Beale Street during the 1930s and 1940s.

The Memphis Arts Festival brings the arts to Tennesseans every fall.

A replica of a famous Greek building in Athens, the Parthenon, stands in Nashville's Centennial Park.

In Nashville, the Grand Ole Opry stages and broadcasts many country-music performances.

Horseback riding is one of the best ways to explore Tennessee's rugged mountain terrain.

SPORTS

Tennessee is a playground for people who enjoy the outdoors. Residents can go mountain biking, hiking, and horseback riding in the state. Water sports, such as fishing and swimming, are also popular. Tennessee boasts more than twenty major lakes and reservoirs, and more than 19,000 miles of streams. Tennessee's official sport fish, the largemouth bass, is one of the most sought-after fish in the state. Its popularity with fishers is due to its strong fighting ability and large size.

The Great Smoky Mountains National Park is a popular destination for outdoor enthusiasts. It is the most visited park in the nation. Located in eastern Tennessee, the Great Smoky Mountains National Park draws more than 9 million people annually. The Paris Landing State Resort Park is located in the Cumberland Plateau. Spelunkers, or cavers, head to this park to explore the many intricate caves in the area. Tennessee has more than 3,800 known caves.

QUICK FACTS

The Ocoee River in southeastern Tennessee is rated among the top rivers in the nation for white-water rafting. It was the site of the white-water kayak competitions in the 1996 Olympic Games.

Tennessee's largemouth bass can be found in most of the lakes and streams in the state.

The Guinness Book of World Records lists the "Lost Sea" in Sweetwater as the largest underground lake in the country.

Tennessee is one of the top hang-gliding locations in the United States.

White-water rafting on Tennessee's major rivers has become a popular adventure sport throughout the state.

Automobile racing is a great spectator sport in Tennessee. The Bristol Motor Speedway has earned a reputation as "The World's Fastest Half-Mile." Recently, seating has been expanded at the Bristol Motor Speedway, from 71,000 seats to approximately 135,000 seats. Darrell Waltrip is Bristol's all-time winner. Waltrip, a resident of Tennessee, has won at the Bristol Motor Speedway a record twelve times.

Tennessee's professional football team is the Tennessee Titans. The team moved to Tennessee in 1997 and plays in Nashville's East Bank Stadium. The Nashville Kats play in the American Football League. The Nashville Predators is the state's National Hockey League team. College sports teams include the Memphis Tigers, the Tennessee Volunteers from Knoxville, and the Vanderbilt Commodores from Nashville.

The Bristol Motor Speedway's total length is approximately 3,800 feet. The speedway is home to a variety of racing events, including monster-truck racing and tractor pulls.

QUICK FACTS

Former Titans running back Earl Campbell was named one of Tennessee's official state heroes.

Gatlinburg, located at the entrance of the Great Smoky Mountains National Park, is one of Tennessee's top snowboarding and skiing locations.

The Women's Basketball Hall of Fame is a popular tourist attraction that celebrates the achievements of women's basketball.

In their first season in the American Football League, the Nashville Kats won ten out of fourteen games.

Brain Teasers

1
Which four cities have served as Tennessee's capital?

Answer: In Tennessee's early history, four different towns served as the seat of government: Knoxville, Kingston, Murfreesboro, and Nashville. Nashville was chosen as the permanent capital city in 1843.

2
How tall does the state tree, the tulip poplar, grow?

Answer: The tulip poplar can reach a height of up to 200 feet.

3
TRUE OR FALSE?

There is a man buried in the Tennessee State Capitol.

Answer: True. The designer of the Capitol, William Strickland, knew that he would not live to see the completion of the building. He asked to be buried in its walls. The Tennessee legislature agreed. His body rests in the north portico of the Nashville building.

4
TRUE OR FALSE?

Cotton is Tennessee's main crop.

Answer: True. Cotton ranks first, with tobacco following closely behind.

5

How many United States presidents were born in Tennessee?

Answer: Three. In 1829, Andrew Jackson was the first president from Tennessee. In 1845, James K. Polk was the second, and, in 1865, Andrew Johnson became the third president from Tennessee.

6

What does "The Meat and Three" mean?

Answer: It is a lunchtime meal that consists of a meat entrée, served with three kinds of vegetables.

7

The town of Shelby is known for making which writing tool?

Answer: The pencil.

8

How did Maxwell House come up with their company motto, "good to the last drop"?

Answer: President Theodore Roosevelt commented that the coffee at the old Maxwell House Hotel in Nashville was "good to the last drop."

FOR MORE INFORMATION

Books

Lacey, Theresa Jensen. *Amazing Tennessee: Fascinating Facts, Entertaining Tales, Bizarre Happenings, and Historical Oddities from the Volunteer State.* New York: Rutledge Hill Press, 2000.

Sirvaitis, Karen. *Tennessee.* Minneapolis: Lerner Publications, 1993.

Thompson, Kathleen, *Tennessee (Portrait of America).* Orlando: Raintree Steck-Vaughn, 1996.

Web Sites

You can also go online and have a look at the following Web sites:

Tennessee Department of Education
www.state.tn.us/education/mstudent.htm

Official Site of the State of Tennessee
www.state.tn.us/

Great Smoky Mountains Information
www.ismoky.com/mountains/history

Some Web sites stay current longer than others. To find other Tennessee Web sites, enter search terms such as "Tennessee," "Nashville," "Memphis" or any other topic you want to research.

GLOSSARY

amendment: a change, usually to a document

assassinated: murdered, often for political reasons

ceded: formally surrendered or given to another

circumference: the outer boundary, especially of a circular area

civil-rights movement: the struggle in the 1950s and 1960s to provide racial equality for African Americans in the United States

hydroelectricity: water-generated power

industrialized: an economy that is largely based upon industry and manufacturing

municipalities: cities, towns, or villages with their own local government

nocturnal: active at night and inactive during the day

precipitation: moisture that falls from the sky, such as rain, snow, or hail

ratify: to approve

rural: relating to the country

tributaries: streams that flow into larger streams or rivers

 INDEX